KU-178-269

Our Class

Michele Paul

Peter is in our class. He has short hair.

short hair

HAPPINESS
HAPPINESS
Frames

Emma is in our class. She has freckles.

freckles

Cleo is in our class. She has brown eyes.

brown eyes

Ryan is in our class. He has red hair.

red hair

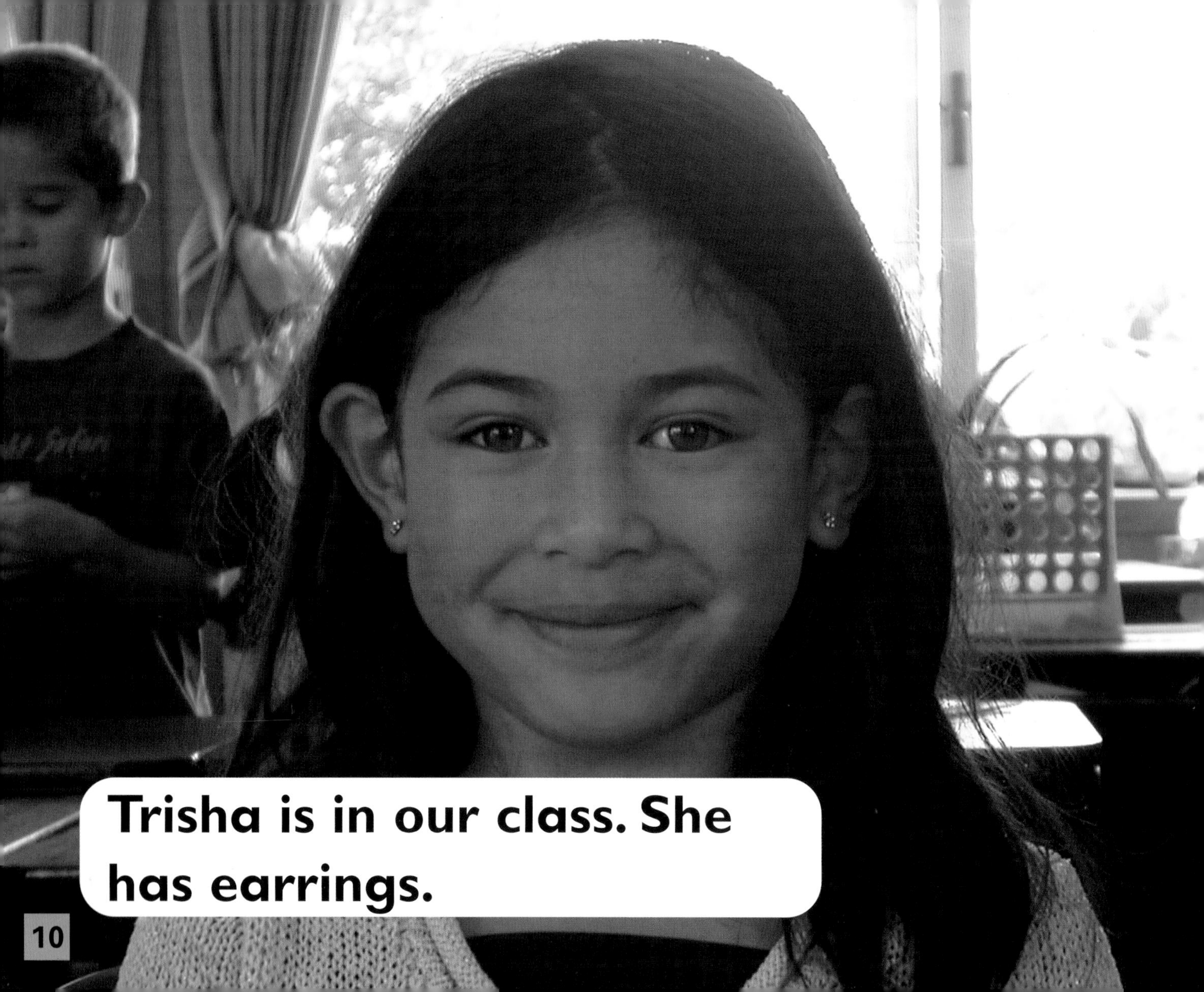

Trisha is in our class. She has earrings.

earrings

Mark is in our class. He has lost a tooth.

lost tooth

Sunita is in our class. She has pigtails.

pigtails

MARLBOROUGH
PRIMARY SCHOOL
ROOM 7 YEAR 2

This is our class.